Poe Motion

Warwickshire
Edited by Annabel Cook

 Young**Writers**

First published in Great Britain in 2004 by:
Young Writers
Remus House
Coltsfoot Drive
Peterborough
PE2 9JX
Telephone: 01733 890066
Website: www.youngwriters.co.uk

SB ISBN 1 84460 380 6

Foreword

This year, the Young Writers' 'Poetry In Motion' competition proudly presents a showcase of the best poetic talent selected from over 40,000 up-and-coming writers nationwide.

Young Writers was established in 1991 to promote the reading and writing of poetry within schools and to the youth of today. Our books nurture and inspire confidence in the ability of young writers and provide a snapshot of poems written in schools and at home by budding poets of the future.

The thought effort, imagination and hard work put into each poem impressed us all and the task of selecting poems was a difficult but nevertheless enjoyable experience.

We hope you are as pleased as we are with the final selection and that you and your family continue to be entertained with *Poetry In Motion Warwickshire* for many years to come.

Contents

Rugby High School

Southam College

Sarah Turner (13)	108
Rosie Lambert (11)	109
Daisy Harrold (11)	110
Adrian van Kesteren (11)	111
Heather Campbell (11)	112
Lauren Case (12)	113
Joanna Green (12)	114
Emma Hill (11)	115
Jennifer Fennell (13)	116
Callum Moffat (11)	117
Annie Allsop (11)	118
Alice Thompson Lane (11)	119
April Gillett (11)	120
Olivia Ballard (11)	121
Jess Pollitt (11)	122
Luke Ashworth (11)	123
Lee Bodfish (12)	124
Ricky Jones (12)	125
Joanna Middleton (11)	126
Emily Howell (11)	127
Jason Heeles (12)	128
Alexandria Kercher (11)	129
Leanne Tarver (11)	130
Jethro Lomas (11)	131
Toby Tomlinson (11)	132

Sparrowdale School

James Handford (13)	133
Michael Cox (13)	134
Shane Bibb (13)	135
Danielle Gallett (13)	136
Jenna Passey (13)	137
Sarah O'Reilly (13)	138
Sabrina Parker (13)	139
Sara Bibb (13)	140
Tom Betteridge (14)	141

The Poems

Disaster Zone

In springtime when the leaves of lofty oaks
Sparkle with diamonds of dew
And the steely grey sky looks ominous,
I stroll across the clumps of bushy emerald grass
And watch the nimble deer scatter.

When summer arrives I wander through the fields spotted
                                    with daisies,
I recline in the sun like a cat and slurp on ice creams by the stream,
Then I lie on the ground and make shapes with the clouds,
Or stare in awe at the silky cobwebs that are home to the spiders.

In autumn, leaves lined with gold fall like delicate fairies from the sky,
The water freezes in the stream and the ground coats itself with frost,
Tiny grey mice scamper through leaves and voles
Create intricate escape plans in the soil.

By winter, the damage has been done,
The chips are twinkling from shattered beer glasses,
The drunkards roll in at night to a beautiful sanctuary and leave
A dangerous minefield of crisp packets, glass and cans.
The next day, rabbits smear their blood across the field,
Leaving their crimson trail behind them.
This disaster zone is no longer a safe place for anyone.

Hannah Mackenzie (13)

Poems

What are light? Feathers and cotton wool.
What are shiny? Suns and stars.
What are long? Roads and snakes.
What are blue? Skies and lakes.

Snakes
Slimy, scaly
Slithering slowly around
Cool, interesting, smooth, long
Wicked!

Scott Warwick (13)

No One Knows!

Secrets flick'ring,
Large and bright,
Secrets flick'ring,
Breaking free.

Secrets laughing,
Loud and clear.
Secrets laughing,
Spilling out.

Secrets creeping,
Small and calm.
Secrets creeping,
Keeping calm.

Secrets running,
Bold and brave.
Secrets running,
Panting hard.

Secrets hiding
Everywhere.
Secrets hiding,
No one knows.

Anthony Williams (13)
Alcester Grammar School

Shapeless

If shapeless is your style,
Then she'd make you smile.
If sideburns are your thing,
Then give her a ring.
If you like an ugly face,
Then it's her you'll embrace.
Of course it's personality
That gives a mutuality.
If you like bores and freaks
Then she only has to speak.
If pretension turns you on
In a second I'll be gone.
But I know she isn't right,
That's why I'm putting up a fight.
I'd treat you like a king,
I know it's the real thing.
So forget her -
Love me.

Jane Shields (17)
Alcester Grammar School

Noisy Jack

The boy called Jack was perching on a tree,
He was resting from doing the housework.
Squatting like a gorilla, thinking hard,
He was going to stay all night.

Jack was giggling to himself,
He was cackling like a magpie up a tree,
Snorting like a camel in the desert,
Jack was sniggering at the people passing by.

Jack was howling like a wolf at the moon,
Wailing with starvation.
He was humming himself to sleep.
Goodnight Jack!

Kieran English, Eddy Sabine, James Batchelor
& Sean Smith (11 & 12)

Brooke School

All About Cats

Cats chase mice to catch them and have fun.
Heart-shaped noses, make you think of love.
When cats are happy they purr,
They sound like an engine, running well.
They sing for their supper with a loud miaow!
They have pointy ears like pyramids.
Cats always run away from me.
Cats are mostly cute and cuddly.
A cat's fur is soft, like a pillow.
Cats like to play hide-and-seek.
Claws that are as sharp as needles.
Cats' whiskers are like toothbrush bristles,
Cats tails are furry and soft, like a feather.
Cats scratch, bite rats,
They wrap around your legs like a scarf.
Almond-shaped eyes looking at you.
At night, cats' eyes are like a silver light.

Class 6E
Brooke School

One To Ten

One wavy, windy wave,
Two trendy teddies talking,
Three tasty teacakes toasting,
Four favourite flavours flowing,
Five Freddies flying funny,
Six slimy snakes slithering,
Seven sleeping sea lions sliding,
Eight elephants eating eggs,
Nine naughty Nellies' night,
Ten tickets traded tonight.

Jade Mazey (14)
Brooke School

Me

When I woke up my head was on fire
The lights were as bright as the sun
I felt my face, it was as smooth as a cue ball
Then rough as sandpaper
My legs felt like stones
My arms like dumbbells
The ward smelt like my nan's house.
Why did I get in that car?
Why? Why? Why?

Tom Hill (13)
Etone School

Britain

A poem, a poem about Britain,
The bumpy hills with sheep and cows grazing.
This poem by myself I have written,
With the Queen sitting on her throne, gazing.

Fresh English breakfasts in a B & B,
And the London Eye, with its pods spinning,
And all the sports, like football and rugby.
The English football team, they are winning.

Looking at her country, she is smiling.
Looking at Big Ben in all its beauty,
And Tony Blair with his phone dialling,
Still the Queen has to fulfil her duty.

So I'll tell her to rock on Windsor!
So I'll tell her to rock on Windsor!

Peter Rowland-Jones (12)
Hartshill High School

Great Britain

Rolling, luscious hills, fields of golden corn,
Trees and shrubs blowing in the wind and rain.
Cars drive past sheep, while lambs are being born.
The black taxies roll down the dusty lane.

English breakfast eaten by everyone.
All the landmarks, like the London Tower.
People on the London Eye in the sun,
Boys playing football, girls picking flowers.

Writers like George Elliot and Shakespeare.
The Queen and the royal family.
Shops sell things by pounds, sometimes it's quite dear.
Great Britain is changing all around me,

Because Great Britain is my home, you see.
Great Britain is changing all around me.

Fawn Harrad (12)
Hartshill High School

Britain

Britain is a populated island,
With lots of different places to visit,
And lots of high mountains and low grassland,
Isn't that a very good place to sit?

There are plenty of attractions to see,
Including the Tower of London and Big Ben,
And other different places, like the sea.
On the farms, there are more sheep than hens.

Almost everybody owns a TV,
The death of Guy Fawkes made bonfire night,
Only the Queen has the secret throne key,
Football hooligans end up in a fight.

So at the end of this beautiful day,
I may come again for another stay.

Vincent Leung (12)
Hartshill High School

Untitled

Rolling, luscious fields filled with sheep and cows,
Little lambs being born every day.
As you look up at the trees they all bow,
And the snow-white baby lambs jump and play.

When you wake up, try an English breakfast,
Then after, try a quick game of football.
When the sun comes, make the most of it, it won't last.
It can be hot, but when it rains, it falls.

To the Tower of London or Big Ben,
To the Houses of Parliament and maybe
You might just see some royal guards, and then,
Britain's Queen and her royal family.

Natalie Harrad (12)
Hartshill High School

Britain, The Sonnet

Come to Britain, it's traditional and cool,
Tower of London, Millennium Dome,
The Queen and Prime Minister rule,
You'll soon make it into your home.

Football, rugby, our favourite sports,
Chicken and sheep on the farm,
Historical sites, Roman forts,
So peaceful and calm.

TV is our favourite thing,
English breakfast served all day,
Watch Pop Idol and see them sing,
June, July, August, May.

So Britain can have a good time,
We're trying our best to clean up crime.

Adam Jones (12)
Hartshill High School

Why?

Why, Britain, have you given into the beasts
That have destroyed you gradually
Year by year, day by day?

The landscape's changing, rearranging,
But what can I do but stand and stare?

Buildings growing all around me.

People thinking, but about what?
How they can make it a better place!

Good thoughts, just bad plans.
Why do we do this to our homes?

Aimmee Kemp (12)
Hartshill High School

The Sad Story

The royal family in their glory
Standing high and proud, while the crowds cry,
The tourists flocked to hear their sad story
And say to the deceased Princess, goodbye.

Everyone will tell you she was refined,
She was kind and helpful to everyone.
We all said she'd never be forgotten
And when she smiled, the whole wide sky shone.

The family were upset at the news
On that fatal day they all found out.
As Princess Diana was bad to lose,
Her sad death was something to think about.

We all miss you, Princess, so very much,
It seemed as if you had the magic touch.

Kailey O'Neill (12)
Hartshill High School

Britain

Rolling, luscious fields filled with green and white,
Whilst the farmer's wife is ploughing the grain,
Sometimes the land isn't a pretty sight,
The grain and wheat grow because of the rain.

The royal family are oh so nice,
The London Eye is very big and round.
The Queen's guards creep around like little mice,
When you ride it you can see the Queen's grounds.

Guns and violence make people so sad,
The violence and crime is on the up.
You wonder if Britain is going mad,
The British police should lock them all up.

The British weather is so cold and wet,
The weather tomorrow is wet, I bet.

Danielle Le-Blancq (12)
Hartshill High School

Great Britain

Rolling, luscious fields of green and white,
Farmers in their fields are watching their flock.
Outside with their eyes open day and night,
Out at night watching their sheep and their clock.

Clouds scattered over the blue, quilted sky,
Light-feathered birds that are flying so high,
Waving at the tractors that pass them by,
Sheep lie under the sky as farmers sigh.

Crop farmers in the golden, waving fields,
Through the years we have invented new ways
To crop, yield and farm to make our beloved meals,
Think of the farmers that work through the days.

Great Britain, you are definitely best,
We love you, you are better than the rest.

Katie McIver (13)
Hartshill High School

Great Britain

Rolling, luscious fields full of cows and sheep,
Lots of baby lambs glad to be alive.
On the road all the cars are going beep,
A race track's where the Aston Martins drive.

The most traditional food's fish and chips,
If you're hungry, get an English breakfast,
HP sauce is the most scrumptious of dips,
But get them quick, because they'll all go fast.

In London in a palace the Queen lives,
The giant London Eye is very high.
Beggars beg for money and worker gives,
The top of Big Ben sits high in the sky.
Shakespeare had a great gift of poetry,
Now the bard lies in a cemetery.

Abigail Chetwynd (12)
Hartshill High School

Sonnet Of Britain

Walking past the sheep and cows in the meadow,
Trekking over the hills of Britain,
Eating the best 50p chips to go,
Oh yes! That's why we love to be British.

England, Ireland, Scotland, Wales are British.
They all make one small place, but it's well known.
Yes, forget Jamaica, we are British,
Britain is the best, because it's my home.

TVRs, Aston Martins and Minis,
These are some of the best of Britain's cars.
Britain is best, even though it's mini,
Britain's Queen even gave us some great bars.

That is why we are British and the best,
Yes, that's why we are British and the best.

Alex Jones (12)
Hartshill High School

Great Britain Is Not That Great

Oh my Great Britain, you're not all that great,
Full of pollution and bad goings on.
There are so many things that I do hate,
Hunting and killing, I wish they were gone.

Car fumes polluting our beautiful isle,
Factories blowing out smelly, dark smoke,
Hunting poor foxes does not make me smile,
Bleeding and dying, it gives us no hope.

Drug dealers hiding in dark alleyways,
Addicts are desperate to pay for their goods,
Killings and muggings, they happen each day,
They get caught and arrested like they should.

Oh my Great Britain, you're not all that great,
Those are the things that I really do hate.

Emily Parr (12)
Hartshill High School

Britain

There's lots to do and see in Great Britain,
London Eye, Madam Tussaud's and Big Ben,
Green-filled fields with sheep dancing in the sun,
Cabs driving round killing old men.

English breakfast, or if it's fish and chips,
There's definitely a taste to suit all.
All the poor sports' people need some good tips,
So come along and kick around a ball.

Don't let the horrible weather get you down,
Plenty of different things to do inside.
Museums, exhibitions, things off ground,
The sand and sea make the beach a great site.

Go and enjoy the greatest fun,
Go to the best place on Earth,
Great Britain!

Lori Stringer (12)
Hartshill High School

Great Britain

Britain is my home and my sanctuary,
No place would I rather be than here, now,
Even though the Queen is old and weary,
She looks over us, to her we will bow.

To some people Britain means politics,
Our horrible weather may make you cringe,
Some people think Britain needs to be fixed,
But to me, Britain means so many things.

Britain is the place where I have grown up,
It's where I hang out will all my friends,
Lots of tea, most British just love a cup,
And there's lots of shops full of different trends.

So many memories stored in my brain,
This is my home, my life, my Britain.

Matthew Moore (12)
Hartshill High School

Britain

This is a poem all about Britain.
Britain made the TVR, what a car.
Romeo and Juliet, Shakespeare had written,
We are the best country by far.

Big Ben, the London Eye, sit on the river,
Buckingham Palace, the house of the Queen,
Millennium Bridge will make you quiver.
A celebrity can always be seen.

Red post boxes are dotted around,
David Beckham plays for our team,
Everywhere you go a pub can be found,
Because we are the best and it's no dream.
I hope you think that England is great,
Because we have lots and lots of mates.

Mitchell Kemp (12)
Hartshill High School

Nice Britain?

Driving through London on a rainy day,
Black cabs whizzing past, down the roads they go.
Winter's thick ice makes them skid on their way,
Children are playing in polluted snow.

I imagine a world that is perfect;
But when I open my eyes, I've got this,
A huge world of houses and skyscrapers,
Why we made it just like this, I don't know.

Before my time, there was great countryside,
Vast fields of sheep grazing in the sun,
Waves of luscious sand along the seaside,
That was the time when it was very fun.

Today we just drive around in our cars,
Giving off pollution everywhere,
Finding cures to diseases that we caused,
And making pleasantries for us to use.

People begging for money from the rich,
Living unfortunate lives on the road.

Curtis Thompson (12)
Hartshill High School

Britain's Countryside

Rolling, luscious fields, full of mustard seeds,
Pearly white sheep, grazing on the green grass,
A pond in the distance, the ducks in the reeds,
People look at windmills as they pass.

The calm smell of a log-burning fire,
All the birds sing in the calm, peaceful winds,
People must come here to retire,
The rain can be calm, or as sharp as pins.

A little girl picks flowers for her mum,
Poppies are wild at the side of the road,
I see butterflies, I hear bees that hum,
By the side of a stream sits an old toad.

Even though Great Britain seems very small,
Even the highest mountain can't see it all.

Elinor Morgans (12)
Hartshill High School

A River's Journey

As I head downstream
My path is not true
Weaving this way and that
I twist and turn
Wandering endlessly.
Ambling along
I flow serenely
Gliding and sliding
Slipping quietly by
Gently lapping my banks.
But as I gather momentum
I start to race and chase
Hurrying, scurrying
Dashing, splashing
And crashing into my sides
I whirl and twirl
And toss and turn
Restlessly.

Jenny Sculpher (12)
Rugby High School

The White Horses

When the moon is all alight,
On the eve of Midsummer's Day,
And the world is quiet for the night,
The white horses come to play.

Out of the sea come one and all
With many a whinny and neigh,
To prance on the beach and have a ball
The white horses come to the bay.

Big horses, young foals, all come ashore
As white as the cliffs are grey,
As fast as the birds who far above soar
The white horses race away.

Round and round, a grand time they spend,
Racing each other to say,
'Such joy, such fun should never end!'
But night is turning to day.

So of their games they are bereft,
'Into the sea!' They gallop away;
And by the morn, hoof prints are all that is left
Of the white horses who came to play.

But when the moon is all alight,
On the eve of Midsummer's Day,
And the world is quiet for the night,
The white horses still come to play.

Jessica Steele (12)
Rugby High School

Silence

Silence is beautiful,
Things can be said through silence,
That have never been heard before.

Silence is wonderful,
No one has ever heard silence,
There is always a drip of a tap,
Or the whistle of a bird.

Silence is great,
You can think when there is silence,
You find out things you never knew before.

Silence is indescribable,
Nobody knows what silence is,
Silence is broken.

Louise Young (12)
Rugby High School

Why?

T oday is the eleventh of September,
W hich is a day we will all remember.
I n the distance there is a rumble,
N o! The Twin Towers begin to crumble.

T ime stands still as they start to fall,
O nce a lovely building, now nothing at all.
W asted lives, we question *why?*
E verybody, everywhere begins to cry.
R elatives and workers together they come,
S urvivors, there are only some.

Emily Webb (12)
Rugby High School

The River Poem

Slowly trickling downstream,
Lapping against the sides.
Tossing, turning, we're picking up a pace,
Now it's turned into a running race.
Nearly at the sea,
What can I see?
Big, crashing waves,
I want to be there first!
Pushing, shoving, beating, bashing,
Now we're here at last.

We're at the sea,
But where should I go,
There's so much to see?
When night falls,
We crush the cliffs,
We tickle the sand
And bring the beach alive!
But in the day,
I can only sway
To people walking by.

Victoria Stanley (12)
Rugby High School

My Water Poem

Drip, drop, splish, splosh, drip, splosh.
People need this wasted water,
Drip, drop, splish, splosh, drip, splosh,
We waste our water just like this.

Jewels on the window
Glistening in the morning sun,
Twinkles on the pavement,
Like sparkling diamonds all day long.

Ripples move gently in
Unsettled puddles on the ground,
With some help from the wind,
Splashing and splishing rain circles round.

Drip, drop, splish, splosh, drip, splosh,
People need this wasted water.
Drip, drop, splish, splosh, drip, splosh,
We waste our water just like this.

Run the tap nice and warm,
Now soak yourself in waters deep,
Glad that you now are clean,
Now back to the ground it must seep.

Journey down to the drain,
First to the river, then the sea,
Clouds made from our puddles,
Make rain to pour on you and me.

Drip, drop, splish, splosh, drip, splosh,
People need this wasted water.
Drip, drop, splish, splosh, drip, splosh,
We waste our water just like this.

Emily Stafford (13)
Rugby High School

Children

Laughing in the playground,
Spinning around and around,
Shouting 'Tig!', chasing each other,
One falls to the ground.

Making a mess with their dinner,
They get it all down their shirt,
Mum will have to clean it up,
Along with the rest of the dirt.

Throwing the ball, then running,
Playing lots of fun games,
And as they pass the ball around,
They call each other's names.

When the school day is over,
They run to Mum and Dad.
'What have you got all down your shirt?
That was *very* bad!'

'Oh Mum, I'm really sorry,
Can you clean it up?'
'Well I really haven't got much choice,
You are a mucky pup!'

When it starts to get dark,
And it's getting late,
They still refuse to go to bed,
Although it's half-past eight!

Rebecca Webb (12)
Rugby High School

RHS (Rugby High School)

The sound of a whisper, so quaint, so strong,
The sound of a sigh, getting a question wrong,
The tickle of a raindrop on the window sill,
The sound of a bell, the classrooms fill.
Phew, the lesson ends in ten minutes' time,
Centenary day singing the anthem in rhyme,
Mr Walker at the front, conducting the choir,
Mrs Lines in the library connecting the phone wire,
Miss Middlehurst in her shorts and a big jumper,
Mrs Forsythe, if you don't sit right, she'll call you a slumper,
The sound of a giggle, a sixth-former passes,
With greasy skin, a spotty face and big, round glasses.
'Bonjour, toute le monde,' Madam Chabert will say,
Or 'Guten tag,' if you're talking to Frau Spray,
Miss Evans in history, the Tudors she'll teach,
Finally the holidays, a chance to lie on the beach.

Hannah Smith (13)
Rugby High School

Autumn Leaves

The crunch of the fallen leaves
Penetrates the silent air
Having left the frosty trees
The branches are left still and bare.

The cold breeze runs through them
As they scatter across the ground
They slowly fly in the wind
To be heaped in a golden mound.

Their colours, crisp and golden
From a green to a shining red
Curling up through their fall
The shrivelled leaves are dead.

Mary van Kesteren (12)
Rugby High School

War

Click, bang another man dead,
Millions of tears being shed.
Bombs racing through the air,
Children sobbing, 'Does anyone care?'

Victims dying for a vital drink,
Life or death on the brink.
Filthy water spreading disease,
Raging through villages like scavenging fleas.

War poisoning minds of innocent ones,
Filling their heads with death and guns.
Destroying their childhood with tragic memories,
Nobody listening to their desperate pleas.

Why not stop this heartache now?
We'll find the answer some way, somehow.
So many children drowning in despair,
No one to love, no one to care.

War devastating the lives of many,
Yet the rich and wealthy will not spare a penny.
Countless people struggling to live,
Please spare a thought, there is still time to give.

Jessica Vaughan (12)
Rugby High School

Water

My pa once said to me, 'Water is rare,
And you don't just run a tap to get it,
But you may have to trek for hours on end,
And to do that takes a lot of spirit.'

He said to treasure the water we have,
Because maybe one day we won't
Have the precious gem given to us,
It maybe a rumour, a saying, or a quote.

My ma once said to me, 'You may not be now,
But one day you will be thankful for what you will have.'
But I'm still waiting for that day
To come and pass.

She also said not to take for granted,
The wish we will want and have had,
I wish I had listened to her then,
And I wouldn't be where I am now.

I was stupid as a child,
Shouting at my parents and grandparents too,
Because now that I am old and wrinkled,
I want to take back what I did do.

My grandparents are long gone,
My parents are now with them,
And I am in need of water,
That really precious gem.

Hannah Plimmer (12)
Rugby High School

Racing River

Gushing along downstream,
Jumping from rock to rock,
The river twists this way and that,
Cool and winding water.

Spinning and twirling forever,
A ballerina dancing delicately,
Wide in places, narrow in others,
Millions of small brooks joining,
All leading towards the sea!

Now flowing faster and rougher,
The pace quickens, the excitement grows,
Spray enters the sky,
Comes plummeting back down again.

Pushing, shoving, competition is rising,
More ferocious every second,
Desperate attempts to overlap,
Over, under and through.

Suddenly, it comes to a halt,
Becomes still, frozen and rigid,
But then a trickle enters the sea,
And the race has only just begun!

Alice Pope   (12)
Rugby High School

Have You Ever?

Have you ever
Looked into your lover's eyes?
Bright and sparkly like a waterfall,
Bright and beautiful,
Bright and special like nothing else . . .

Have you ever
Looked into your soul?
So deep with feelings,
So twisted with deceit,
So lost with life . . .

Have you ever
Had hopes and dreams
That get through to your heart,
That make you seem as though you're on top of the world,
That let your mind wander to far-off places . . . ?

Have you ever
Lived for today?
A special feeling that gets you every day,
A feeling that gets you flying high,
A thought that you never know what is coming next . . .

Well I want
To see those bright sparkling eyes,
And see into my soul,
And have those hopes and dreams,
And live for today,
That's all I want and that's how I want to be!

Alice Spiby (13)
Rugby High School

People Can Be . . .

People can be
As mad as a hatter
That jumps on my bed,
It could've been a rabbit
Or a hare instead.

As stiff as a board
That lays under my bed,
As mighty as a sword
From a knight I might wed.

As smelly as socks
On hot sweaty feet,
As boring as flocks
Of meandering sheep.

As happy as a Larry,
The boy next door,
He tells me he's called Harry,
Oh what a bore.

As bossy as my mum
When I stop out late,
She's the only one
Who says, 'Be back at eight.'

As loud as a whistle
Blown right in your ear,
As big as that thing in Brighton,
Oh yes that's right - the pier.

People can be annoying
And sometimes really nice.
And if they are really moody
You should always think twice!

Hannah Reilly (12)
Rugby High School

Visit To A War Cemetery

They lie there in the garden,
Visited day by day
By their loved ones,
Friends and strangers.

They lie there,
English soldiers on foreign ground,
All gravestones look the same,
But each one is as individual as the next.

They lie there,
The flowers sway in the breeze,
The bushes rustle
And the gravestones stand proud.

So remember
Those brave soldiers
Who died for us,
Long ago.

Sarah Cook (11)
Rugby High School

Rugby High School

RHS is full of people who greet you with a big smile every day.
RHS is full of people who every day say,
Hello or how are you? That's what they'll say.
They can talk to you when you are sad
Or look after you when you are ill.
When you forget your dinner money then
They'll even foot the bill.

RHS is such a good place but nobody knows it
As much as you or I do.
You see everyone thinks that it is a snobby school,
But really it's just like any other.
I know that and I hope that you do now too.

Hannah Rickaby (12)
Rugby High School

The Big, Blue and Greeny Sea

The big, blue and greeny sea,
Sometimes rough, sometimes calm,
Always very salty and wet,
The big, blue and greeny sea.

The big, blue and greeny sea
Stretches as far as the eye can see,
Always flowing wave by wave,
The big, blue and greeny sea.

The big, blue and greeny sea,
Underneath the flowing waves
Coral and fish hide in their caves,
In the big, blue and greeny sea.

The big, blue and greeny sea,
Rocks and fossils what no one can see,
Not even fish or coral can reach them
At the bottom of the big, blue and greeny sea.

Lucy Owen (11)
Rugby High School

Friendship

I used to think life wasn't fair,
That it puts us through more than we could bear.
But now I know that was wrong,
I know that it has been so long.
I just wanted to tell you that you're my friend.

Amy Wilson (11)
Rugby High School

Flower Garden

Splashes of colour,
Pink, yellow, red,
Daffodils, lilies, roses
In the flower bed.

Swaying gently
In the breeze,
Tall, slender stalks
And fragile green leaves.

Soft-coloured petals
Or dainty and white,
You can have any colour
Pale or bright.

Flowers are beautiful,
Flowers are fair,
But whatever you do
Just leave them there.

Susannah Tarrant (11)
Rugby High School

The Darkness

Falling like a deep blue cloak over the town,
Quicker and quicker, fast to come down,
The day has gone, it is almost night,
Now there is almost no trace of light.

The night is so dark it is almost black,
You almost think the light won't come back,
Outside it's so cold you almost freeze,
Although there's not the slightest breeze.

The sun is just peeping through the trees
And the light is coming back with ease,
Now the sun is shining bright again
And no strand of the darkness remains.

Amelia Walsh
Rugby High School

The Sea

The sea is a place where seagulls fly,
Sometimes low, sometimes high.
On stormy days people flee
From the great, furious and unhappy sea.
But on calm days the sea is kind
And on these days you will find
That more people go there to play
On a beautiful, warm summer's day.

Neha Parmar (11)
Rugby High School

In The Sky

The sun, bright, beaming and hot,
Making people stop a lot.
So hot it's burning every ground,
It's always turning us round and round.

Clouds, big, fluffy and white,
Completely out of sight.
Gently soaring through the sky,
Way, way, way up high.

Rain, wet, hard and soft,
Hear it thundering on the loft.
The grass is greener than ever before,
In England rain comes more and more.

Moon, sad, happy and light,
Its shiny rays brighten up the night.
It drifts so slowly through the sky,
Always looking at you eye to eye.

Stars, sparkle, glow and shine,
All the planets say, 'That star is mine.'
They all have lives like a little critter,
Up in the sky they just glitter and glitter.

Everything moving by and by,
All in motion in the sky.

Megan Turner (11)
Rugby High School

School Experiences

Bubbling and burning,
Mixing and stirring,
Watching and waiting,
All these belong to
A scintillating science lab.

Adding, subtracting,
Timesing and dividing,
Calculators tapping,
All these belong to
A motivating maths room.

Dancing, running,
Throwing, catching,
Hockey sticks flying,
All these things belong to
A springy sports lesson.

Making, mending,
Cutting, sewing,
Designing and drawing,
All these belong to
A tantalising technology block.

Fascinating form tutors,
Funky friends too,
This makes school a brilliant
Place to educate and
Learn!

Amy Suddens (11)
Rugby High School

Pink And Fluffy

When I do not care
For what the teacher has to say
I put my head upon my hands
And my mind takes me away.

For there is a private place
Especially for me,
I'm the only one who's been there,
It's the land of Pink and Fluffy.

There are many creatures there
That you have never seen,
'Cause they live in Pink and Fluffy
And I'm the only one who's been.

See the stripy trablewacker,
His toes so long and pink.
And there's the hopping ninger tinger
Whose one foot really stinks.

There's a fluffy elephat
Flying overhead!
By my foot a podgy pouffle
Looking sweet until it's fed.

But, alas, I have to go now,
I have to fly away,
I need to know what's going on,
That's enough dreaming for today.

But I know that if I do not care
For what the teacher has to say
I can put my head upon my hands
And my mind takes me away.

Jennifer Louise Simmons (11)
Rugby High School

I Wish . . .

I wish that my dreams would come true,
I wish I could fly to the moon,
I wish that I could walk on the rainbow.

I wish I could swim with dolphins,
I wish I could talk to lions,
I wish that I could ride on an elephant.

I wish that I could sleep on the clouds,
I wish I could see an alien from Mars,
The greatest wish of all,
I wish my wishes would come true.

Toni O'Toole (11)
Rugby High School

It's Christmas

It's Christmas!
Snow is glowing,
Red cheeks are showing,
Sleigh bells are ringing,
The choir is singing.

It's Christmas!
Icicles falling,
Children calling
For their sweets and treats
And Santa Claus stopping at all the streets.

It's Christmas!
Children sleeping,
Slightly peeping,
Santa's coming,
Loudly humming.

It's Christmas!

Sophie Wright (11)
Rugby High School

Hallowe'en

The time has come for Hallowe'en,
When children dress up in frightening attire,
To carry out their tricks and their treats,
No one escapes on this old street.

Ghosts and goblins, monsters a-plenty,
So frightening and terrifying yet comical too,
As they stand at your door with their contorted masks,
Waiting patiently to perform their task.

Mums have been busy carving pumpkins galore,
Sweets and cakes baked ready for bribes,
Bats and bright skeletons hang round the room,
Creaks and cackles in the still night boom.

A time for celebrations for witches and wizards,
When dust is swept from forgotten broomsticks,
To fly and soar in the moonlight as a bat,
Or to stalk your prey as a big black cat.

Children believing the celebration is theirs,
For gaining a multitude of treasure and treats,
Witches and wizards, goblins and dwarves begin to meet,
Knowing the party will only begin as the children sleep.

Katie Windridge (11)
Rugby High School

Sounds Of The School

Creaking of chairs,
Scratching of pens,
Rustling of books,
These are the sounds of the English block.

Hissing of gas,
Squeaking of chalk,
Scraping of chairs,
These are the sounds of the science lab.

Honk of trumpets,
Scales of pianos,
Chiming of triangles,
These are the sounds of the music centre.

Murmurs of voices,
Thudding of footsteps,
Shuffling of bags,
These are the sounds of the school.

Katy Outhwaite (11)
Rugby High School

The Barn Owl

A silent hunter
With swift, soft, feathered wings.
In flight, she has
The appearance
Of a ghostly, pale phantom
Haunting the fields, woods and countryside.

With a tiny rustle
She lifts off the branch
And with her sharp eyes
Scans the ground as she flies over
Looking for mice or voles or any rodent
That could be a tasty meal.

Aha! A movement in the grass
She wheels round and continues to watch.
Then, all of a sudden, she swoops down
Fast and low
Giving the wretched mouse no chance to escape
Her deadly talons.

Such is the life of a barn owl.
Beautifully blood-red.

Caitlin Spencer (12)
Rugby High School

I Remember My Days In Primary School

I remember my days in primary school
From little tot to big girl
From playing with toys to taking tests
From screaming like we were scared to shouting like we were infants.
I remember my days in primary school
From pencil to pen
From small playground to big playground
From starting to leaving
When you're older you change schools
But I remember my days in primary school.

Beccy Setchell (11)
Rugby High School

As The Sun Rises . . .

As the sun rises . . .
Overland birds begin to sing,
On the sea ships emerge from the silent mist,
In the air planes fly from darkness into light,
And in the houses parents begin to wake their sleepy children.

As midday approaches,
The sun is beaming down,
Children are playing and messing around,
Whilst animals in the jungle are seeking cover,
Waiting, waiting until it gets cooler.

Gradually the day draws to a close,
Workers return and children get ready for bed,
And so the sun begins to set,
But on the other side of the world . . . the sun is rising.

Jennifer Stow (11)
Rugby High School

My Thinking Spot

Nobody goes to my spot
they don't even know it's there

My spot is hidden
by a droopy, weeping willow

It's where I go to cry
it's where I go to laugh

My thinking spot
is where I go to let my feelings out

My thinking spot's a secret
so no one knows I'm there

It gives me space to clear my mind
it gives me time to think

My thinking spot will always be
a special place just for me.

Katie Washington (11)
Rugby High School

Why?

What do we want from the world?
Some people want peace,
Some people want love,
Some people want equality.

Why then can't all these people find that and be happy?
Why then do they have to try and get more and more and more?
Some people have nothing.
Why do they have to be greedy, if they have what they want?
Why?
Because they want it all.

But some people have nothing.
No food,
No water,
No equality.

No love.

Charlie Starley (11)
Rugby High School

Depths Of Despair

The spirit of sorrowfulness dwells where I am
All I see is worry and nerve when I look around with sorrowful eyes
The air is choked with misery and dejection
A pit of despair punches my devastated heart
Downcast thoughts fill my rejected mind
Despair and misery sweep over me like waves on a beach
Anxiousness is all around
Swallowed in a dark world of dejection and wrath
I cry out, but get no answer
Is there nowhere to hide from all this tragic
Despair and misery?

Emily Spademan (11)
Rugby High School

Daily Sounds In School

In the ICT room I can hear . . .
Mice clicking,
Keyboards tapping,
Monitors humming,
Printers buzzing.

In the technology block I can hear . . .
Hammers banging,
Saws grinding,
Drills moaning,
Scissors chopping.

In the main hall I can hear . . .
Money jingling,
Girls nattering,
Chairs scraping,
Children munching.

In the music room I can hear . . .
Drums thumping,
Clarinets squeaking,
Maracas rattling,
Chimes chiming.

In the science lab I can hear . . .
Chalk screeching,
Gas taps hissing,
Chemicals bubbling,
Test tubes clanking.

In the dining hall I can hear . . .
Plates smashing,
Food crunching,
Tills tinkling,
Forks scraping.

In the maths department I can hear . . .
Calculators tapping,
Pens scratching,
Paper rustling,
Rulers clicking.

In the art room I can hear . . .
Paint brushes sweeping,
Erasers rubbing,
Paint sloshing,
Paper tearing.

Waiting for the bus I can hear . . .
Teachers shouting,
Children chatting,
Buses screeching to a halt,
Silence, everyone has gone.

Katy Wyton (11)
Rugby High School

The Middle Of The Night

I'm walking through the woods
It's the middle of the night
It's all so very scary
With creatures that can bite

I'm very, very lost
Have I been this way before?
And the leaves are all rustling
On the forest floor

Then I hear a noise
It chills me to the bone
Do I move from here?
Run from this danger zone?

I peer into the dark
Look for the safe way out
The noise comes again
Chilling me throughout

Suddenly I'm running
As fast as an arrow
There's no turning back
My escape was narrow

I stumble upon a cottage
With a little yellow door
I tap on the knocker
With a fancy décor

Then the door creaks open
'Hello, who's there?' I call
Then I see an angry bear
I run, then trip, then fall

I run away again
Like I've never run before
Then I'm in my hometown
And my feet are very sore

I race up to my house
And burst into the room
Mum stands up, *'Where have you been?'*
My dad's face is full of gloom

'Go to bed you naughty girl!'
My misery is deep
I climb into my coffin . . .
Us vampires need our sleep.

Charlotte Wild (11)
Rugby High School

When You're Small

It's fun being one,
Strange though, a man with teddy bear fur on his face keeps
                                        flashing at me,
With a little black box that makes light.
A lady keeps gurgling in my face too, sounds like gurgle
                                        to me anyway.
Adults, they just never grow up,
Playing with toys and pretending spoons are cars,
Honestly.

It's poo being two.
That lady, she is just so pathetic, amazed because I can say, 'Mama.'
I could have said that any day!
Well, she thinks that a magic touch will make a cut better!
Grown ups, will they ever learn?
Thinking I'm a miracle baby just because I can toddle,
Seriously.

Devawn Wilkinson (12)
Rugby High School

Summer Sunset

Like a blazing fire in one's heart you burn,
And darkness falls on your surroundings,
But even still, your beauty challenges anything, everything.
We desire you, long for you, plead for you,
Quarrels are forgotten in your presence.

But when you've gone, the world sleeps,
And once awake, people's lives return to normal.
Until twilight, once again their hearts melt in your presence,
We long for you once more,
The summer sunset of our world.

Vicki Tomlin (11)
Rugby High School

Caged

Encaged inside, the metal bars surround me,
faded memories of where I used to be.
Something inside me wants to burst out,
run wild back to freedom and to shout.
I can't remember freedom anymore,
I'm trapped, there's no escape, not even a door.

Faces looming in from every angle, sneering,
they laugh, they point and they are peering.
The iron floor is nearly as cold as their hearts,
they don't know what I'm suffering or how I was dragged apart.
Dragged apart from freedom and happiness,
those I love I remember even less.

In the land I used to live in, happiness would surround me,
but now I'm lost and concrete is all I see.
So next time you go to the zoo,
don't just think of shops and candy too,
think of me - one lonely lion,
trapped behind these bars of iron.

Abigail Thornton (11)
Rugby High School

A Wish

A wish can be for anyone,
How smart, how pretty, how shy.
A wish can be for anyone,
For someone when they die.

A wish is very easy,
All you do is think.
A wish is very easy,
It's over in a blink.

Florence Thornton Weeks (11)
Rugby High School

The Cat That Got The Cream

The black cat sighed as he gazed at the stars,
How he longed to explore the moon and Mars.
Where he lived, nothing happened at all,
The only thing he could play with was a big, round ball.

So he plotted and planned to make a scheme,
Which would make him the cat that got the cream!
And finally he finished in a month and a day,
It would surely let him get away!

He designed a dummy to take his place,
A mechanical cat that could even chase.
In it he programmed all his usual habits,
From eating to sleeping to chasing rabbits.

No one would notice he was gone;
Oh, how he'd chuckle and sing a song.
He'd dance around till his feet felt sore,
(Sorry, I forget he's a cat, he's got paws.)

That very night, he sneaked out of bed,
And silently said to himself in his head:
I've done it this time, how clever I am,
I'll leave the Earth and take off with a bam!

He climbed into his rocket made only last week
But all of a sudden he felt very weak.
'What's happening?' he cried to himself,
As he sank to the floor moaning like an elf.

He was woken by the vet in the early morning,
The cat was so tired he couldn't stop yawning.
The only explanation of what happened that night,
Is that he was so scared of leaving home, he suffered severe fright!

Beatrice Xu (11)
Rugby High School

A Dream . . .

To be a rat would be such fun
I often wish that I were one

Rats don't have to wash their hands
They run around in happy bands

They dance in mud and play with you
Nobody tells them what to do

And rats don't have to be polite
Or even go to bed at night

But life is risky for a rat . . .
Perhaps I'd rather be a cat.

Sarah Osborne (11)
Rugby High School

New School

I was walking up to the entrance,
Everything was going through my mind,
Cars whizzing past,
Road diggers, digging holes in the ground.
I got into the building,
Voices everywhere,
My heart thumping,
I got into the hall,
Silence.
Nothing but my own footsteps,
Even the creak of a door made me jump.
Outside again,
The door opened.
I'm in my classroom.

Rachel Atkins (11)
Rugby High School

The Moon

The moon is round,
Like a big white ball
Floating on the sea.

You look up high,
So high in the sky . . .
The moon looks like a pea!

A ball of white,
Up in the night
Just big enough to see.

But in real life, it's bigger,
Bigger than a pea.
It doesn't look it from a distance,
But it's bigger than you and me!

Meg Ainsworth (11)
Rugby High School

Moonlight

Silvery light glinting bright
Upon a sheet of blue
White outlines she gently shines
Silently down to you.

She always writes her signature
On the silhouettes of night
With a silver pen she signs her name
In shimmering beams of light.

Heavenly sparkling, she's always there
And stars are all around
She talks to you with gentle voice
And hardly makes a sound.

If you look out of the window tonight
You'll see her very soon
A beautiful, wonderful, heavenly thing
The shining, silver moon.

Emily Burt (11)
Rugby High School

That's The Way It Should Be!

When I was just a little child,
I asked my mother, 'Why?
Why do people fall in love?
And why can't humans fly?'

My mum stopped still and turned around,
And then replied to me,
'That's the way it should be, my love,
That's the way it should be.'

'Why is day always day
And night is always night?
Why is dark so very dark,
And light so very light?'

My mum smiled and began to laugh,
And then she said to me,
'That's the way it should be, my dear,
That's the way it should be.'

'Why the early morning sunshine?
Why the twinkle in the stars?
Why do humans live on Earth,
And not the moon or Mars?'

Yet again my mum looked round,
And said, 'Listen to me,
That's the way it should be, alright?
That's the way it should be!'

One day my sister was asking,
'Why am I just me?'
There was only one thing I could say,
'That's the way it should be!'

Anna Sampson (12)
Rugby High School

Home Alone

When I'm at home and I'm all alone
I can hear the floorboards creaking
I can imagine the burglars seeking
I want this to end
I need my friends
My mum and dad have gone out
I need to scream and shout
I can see pictures upon the curtains
And my dad's tie which he got from Burtons
Then I hear a bang at the door
Why does it have to go on even more?
Who could it be?
I go downstairs towards the door
Making sure I'm still on the floor
I open the door cautiously
And I am grateful to see
My mum and dad standing there
Now I don't have to be, or feel all alone.

Katherine Ronnie (12)
Rugby High School

A Teardrop

As I sit in the dark, damp room, I can see children everywhere
crying for their dead parents.
I can also see parents who are mourning the death of their children.
A teardrop is in everyone's eyes;
the only thing that they have the strength to do.
One candle is lit, the only source of light they own.
Yet this doesn't last and it soon plunges them
into darkness once again.
Suddenly gunshots can be heard somewhere outside
the old, crumbling building.
A single teardrop falls silently to the hard, cold floor.
Everyone suddenly tightens their grip on one another for comfort.
These people don't want war, they want the peace and joy
they once used to share;
before it was snatched away from their soulless bodies.
They want a teardrop of joy and happiness.

Ciara Walsh (12)
Rugby High School

The Pipe Burst

The sun is like a flame,
   Reddening and burning the backs of many.
      The stars are visible at night,
   Like a thousand mini suns.
The breeze isn't relieving,
   And there isn't a cloud in sight.
      Imagine a cloud, imagine a drip,
   Imagine a stream, imagine a river,
Imagine a sea, imagine an ocean.
   It would be bliss, cool water trickling down the burning throat.
   A crash, a bang, a flood of silver.
The wet, sweet taste of water like never before.
   The Earth is blue, blue and cool.
      The world is happy with a sweet taste of never before.
   Next year will be the year when the Earth
Blooms with sweet pink flowers.
   White roses that were never to be seen again.

   The world is glad the pipe burst.

Anna Hobson (13)
Rugby High School

English Weather

The sun glowed down on children's skin,
The heat was seen in waves,
Like sea on the shore,
But still no water came.

Their heads spun,
Not having had a drink to quench their thirst,
Dreaming dangerously, closing eyes,
Hiding the sun, leaving black,
Just black, cool, refreshing black.

The sun looked like a ball of fire,
All alone in the sky,
It is joined by a rain cloud,
Then two, then three, then four.

Now water is here,
Finding a smile on every face,
Everyone celebrates!

Tomorrow everyone will be sad again,
Dreaming of a summer's day,
And so it goes on,
We are never pleased,
We moan, we groan,
English weather.

Hanna Moore (13)
Rugby High School

Wish For Wetness

A curtain veils the sunny weather
Wind blows an icy chill

Suddenly the clouds fly away
The glare blinds the naked eye
Sunglasses are decked
Bright smiles on every face, for miles and miles around
Joyous screams of delight
Suncream spread thick and thin throughout the ages
The sky, blue as the sea
The ground, a cracked brown mosaic

But soon the novelty wears thin
And mothers nurse fiery shoulders
Heat sears like an open oven
Children wish for wetness
Lasts for many weeks
And the weak are burnt at the stake.

Emily Moss (12)
Rugby High School

England

The misty and smoky cloud
covers the magical moon,
casting darkness throughout the night.

Days hold less hope
ashen, overcast skies
hover above soggy, sodden grass.

Wet rain is their neighbour,
a dismal, unwelcome neighbour,
whilst sun is just a distant memory.

The atmosphere of the people,
as colourless as the murky,
dismal skies.

All of a sudden,
eyes quickly glare,
up to the plains of blue,
screens of metal-grey gloom glide open,
revealing a heaven
of thriving, golden light,
cleansing all troubles away.

Charlotte Kertrestel (12)
Rugby High School

Sunshine!

The bright, blazing sun glares down to the villagers.
You are always in need of sunglasses.
Everyone's skin is a deep red and peeling,
It's so hot.

Children yell as their feet touch the burning sand,
You wait so long for a curtain of rain but it never comes.
'Hope' is not a word,
If it is, then why is it so hot still?

Suddenly, a black cloud falls upon the village,
A gust of wind rumbles,
The dry sand cracks like an egg.
Men, women, children come out,
The sky instantly changes colour,
So does the heat.

A cold breeze sweeps over sweaty bodies,
There is a cheer of relief,
Everyone's happy!

Hollie Lynch (12)
Rugby High School

First Day At School!

Up at six,
Soon ready to go,
One hour left,
What to do, don't know.

In the car,
Butterflies appearing,
School in sight,
Bravery disappearing.

Standing in the hall,
Not knowing anyone,
Kids swarming around,
All I wanted was to run.

Standing in the classroom,
Everyone looking at me,
Suddenly all the kids start to chant,
'Good morning Mrs Tree.'

As soon as that was over,
I was ready to start,
Only six and a half hours to go,
But next lesson is art!

Joanna Crowhurst (11)
Rugby High School

Fire!

I warm you in the darkest nights,
I demolish buildings not in fright.
You long for me to fulfil your needs,
But if used carelessly I will sweep what's beneath.

Red, orange and yellow are my cloaks,
Petrifying women, children and folks.
I swiftly spread transforming everything to ash,
Beware, whatever you have will be blackened in a flash.

The smell that I carry will surely not please,
And fumes that I raise are very damaging.
I will persecute anything that is in my way,
I can burn, injure and peel your body.

You may see me as a shining light,
But my personality is not so bright.
I may leave you in dismay,
And comfort you in a wonderful way.

How exquisite I may look,
My only enemies are streams and brooks.
I apologise for how I am,
Causing firefighters to come and get me, again and again.

Sandra Fahmy (11)
Rugby High School

The Adventures Of Mrs Block

William's teacher was called Mrs Block,
Who once turned up in a frilly pink frock.
Everyone laughed and some boys were sick,
The kids were so loud, she hit them with a stick.
'Stop it children, just shut up,
Or else I'll feed you to my pup!'
William, William didn't worry,
He didn't even scream or scurry.
He threw Mrs Block into the bin,
And all the children went home with a grin.

One day Mrs Block took the class for a hike,
Although she herself, she rode on a bike.
They came to a river and sat down for lunch,
When suddenly there came a massive *crunch!*
In Mrs Block's lettuce there had been a snail,
She gave a loud shout, then a small wail.
'Why me?' she asked. 'I'm not even French.'
She sat down heavily on the bench.
Then with a flop - bump, and a howl like a hound,
She slid off her seat and fainted on the ground.

The OFSTED inspector was due in a day,
Mrs Block said, 'I have something important to say.
I hope tomorrow you'll all behave well,
Although this inspection I know will be hell.'
But it's sad to report that the very next day,
The men in white coats came and took her away.
The kids sat in silence in the darkened classroom,
Then a booming voice cut through the gloom.
'Sit down children, I am now your teacher as well as headmaster.'
The day had turned out to be a total disaster.

Katherine Durkin (12)
Rugby High School

Guide Camp

We're going on a Guide camp,
We're going to pitch a tent,
There are twenty of us,
We're going to have some fun.

Uh oh!
Julia's forgotten her sleeping bag.

We're going on a Guide camp,
We're going to pitch a tent,
There are nineteen of us,
We're going to have some fun.

Uh oh!
It's a fifteen-seater minibus.

We're going on a Guide camp,
We're going to pitch a tent,
There are fifteen of us,
We're going to have some fun.

Uh oh!
Traffic jam, one gets out to see what all the fuss is about.

We're going on a Guide camp,
We're going to pitch a tent,
There are fourteen of us,
We're going to have some fun.

Uh oh!
No food, stop at Tesco's, two get out.

We're going on a Guide camp,
We're going to pitch a tent,
There are twelve of us,
We're going to have some fun.

Uh oh!
Rain. We can't pitch a tent!

Melissa Dawson (11)
Rugby High School

Storm

A low growl,
Rumbling threateningly in the air.
A sudden flash,
Illuminating the destruction.
A howling gale,
Whipping ferociously at the man's coat.

The storm tears fiercely at the rocky coastline,
Forcing the waves into icy peaks.
Galloping white horses,
Charging at the craggy bay,
Bursting into sprays of silvery droplets.

The storm rages recklessly on.

Kirsten Evans (12)
Rugby High School

Water

Swiftly rippling as stones are flicked,
Gently streaming down rocky cliffs,
I can be fierce at times,
When I turn to the colour lime!

Stronger than fire, I demolish houses,
Bringing with it comforting couches,
Gentle at moments, when I trickle down streets,
Trying to beware of electric greets!

Oozing through your fingertips,
And springing from your lips,
Enjoying tourists cruising on ships,
As I lash out with whips!

In the oceans and seas,
I contain weeds and reeds,
With soaring dolphins that roam the ocean bed,
And sharks that dolphins dread!

Saba Ali (11)
Rugby High School

Dancing

I dance all day,
I dance all night,
Dance, dance, dance.

I dance while I sleep,
I dance in my dreams,
Dance, dance, dance.

I dance up and down,
I dance this way and that,
Dance, dance, dance.

I dance while I eat,
I dance in the street,
Dance, dance, dance.

I dance with my mum,
I dance with my dad,
Dance, dance, dance.

I dance all day,
I dance all night,
Dance, dance, dance.

Kate Evans (11)
Rugby High School

Noises

People cheering,
Athletes running,
Race drivers steering,
People shouting.

People laughing,
Professionals jumping,
Riders performing,
People eating.

People exhausted,
Racers finished,
Prizes given,
Everyone off home.

Silence finally,
It's time to guess,
Where do you think they are?
Go on have a guess?

Answer: at races and games.

Kathryn Balloch (11)
Rugby High School

School . . .

People laughing,
Coughing and talking,
Teachers teaching,
Students walking.

The buzz of electric,
Wind in the trees,
The zooming of traffic,
And jangling of keys.

The copier copies,
People on phones,
Chairs scratching in classrooms,
We wait to go home . . .

Naomi Bass (11)
Rugby High School

Live In Hope

My children,
Your children,
The children of the land,
They could live in a good world,
If we all lent a hand.

But I won't,
You won't,
No one really cares,
Argue with the government?
No one really dares.

I don't,
You don't,
Not a soul in the population,
It we don't start to think soon,
We'll lose the entire nation.

I'll lose it,
You'll lose it,
Everyone will lose,
The world's a big disaster,
Just listen to the news.

But I can't,
You can't,
I don't think we could cope,
But keep on dreaming, don't give up,
'Cause we all live in hope.

Emily Hewett (13)
Rugby High School

A Classroom

The teacher's voice echoes through the classroom
Like the raging sea tearing at the ragged rocks,
Terrified whimpers, then the soft pattering of pencils on paper,
Silence settles in the classroom, brains tick and pencils write,
Eyes gaze up at the clock which seems to have stopped,
Outside the sea of green grass beckons under the blazing sun,
The teacher prowls the classroom, pouncing on unsuspecting pupils,
Wary eyes follow her progress as beads of sweat
Trickle down foreheads,
Murmurs are sharply banished by the pop-eyed teacher,
Slowly a shaking, quivering hand rises into the air,
'Please Miss . . .'

Charlotte Farthing (11)
Rugby High School

The Planet Of Blue

She drips from the gutters,
Clean and pure,
She comes down from the sky
Keeps us alive.

She is what we need,
The vital thing in our life,
We use her to wash,
And to survive.

She feeds the plants,
Which make oxygen,
We then breathe in their sweet fresh air,
And we stay alive.

She looks after our pets,
Dogs, cats and everything else,
It doesn't matter what you do,
She is always there for you.

When you've been sporty,
She cools you down,
Who is she? you might wonder,
Take a guess . . .

She is water!

Natasha Enticott (11)
Rugby High School

A Potion For Love And A Potion For Revenge

A Potion For Love:

Take a spoon of your love,
And a spoon from theirs,
A pinch of fondness,
And a dash of care,
Then mix with honesty,
The feather of a dove,
You now have the potion,
To have the one you love.

A Potion For Revenge:

Take a pinch of hate,
And a bit of spite,
And the essence of the one,
You wish to fight.
Get a few balled fists,
Add to a spoonful of tears,
Mix thoroughly and spread.
You are now at the top of their list of fears.

Franchesca Branston (11)
Rugby High School

It's Not Fair

Ma comes in to get me out of bed,
I don't want to go to school today,
I want to stay asleep just like my ted.
It's not fair.

I pull on my shirt and a button falls off,
My socks are dirty,
My new watch has just stopped.
It's not fair!

I sit at the breakfast table and eat my food,
My cornflakes are soggy,
Both my sisters are in a mood.
It's not fair!

I trudge out of our home door,
My bag strap breaks,
My books scatter around on the unclean floor.
It's not fair!

It's the worst lesson first,
I really do hate maths,
It's very boring with Mrs Hurst.
It's not fair!

I sit down with my lunch cold and alone,
I open my box but nothing is there,
I see Liz eating and I can't help but groan.
It's not fair!

Next lesson is gym, I detest it a lot,
I wish I were really fit,
So then I wouldn't get sweaty and hot.
It's not fair!

I'm home at last and see my ma,
She looks at me carefully and asks me,
'Do you want a chocolate bar?'
It's n . . . ooh yes please!

Katherine Cory (12)
Rugby High School

A Recipe For Jo

Take a wad of laughter
Add an ounce of fun,
Pour in a litre of music
And love of the sun.

Add a kilo of happiness
And a sprinkle of intelligence,
Just a dash of anger
And a load of confidence.

Mash in a pound of solitude
And a drop of bad moods,
Add 200 grams of animals
And love of all foods!

The result - Jo!

Joanne Bowen (11)
Rugby High School

Dehydrated Disaster

The orange sun is a ball of
intense heat.
A water thief, peeling cracked skin from
deep red backs.
The rivers and streams are bone-dry, frazzled flowers wilted.
The whole city is a dehydrated disaster, everyone is waiting
for the clouds to break, the sky to rumble.
The whole city, dry thirst-quenched desolated area, waiting . . .
Then all of a sudden, the sky makes a loud roar,
The rain is here.

Ruby Kendall (12)
Rugby High School

Oasis

The scene was empty,
as was the sky.
All but the fire flower,
blazing, pounding, scorching
the land.

The sand beneath her,
the sky above,
and all around was emptiness.

But as she walked a tree emerged,
growing lush and tall,
underneath a splash of blue.

The crawl turned into a walk,
into a stumble, into a scramble,
into a run.
The blue turned into a pool.
A blessing from above.

She knelt by the still sheet
and cupped her hands into the liquid silver.
Smiled.
Droplets escaped her grasp,
the diamonds fell,
the still sheet rippled.

The mirage sank back down,
    the oasis gone,
    the blessing no more.

Vanda Pickup (12)
Rugby High School

Water

The sun shone brightly down
    Leaving a trail of sultry rays behind.
Just a drop of water would have sufficed.
    The children gathered around the gateway to the well
Just waiting for water to detonate.
    Suddenly there was water,
And life had been given back!

Latisha McKenzie   (12)
Rugby High School

Wilted

Rose, sweet and pink
Now dry, wilted and dead.

The sun like a flame
Flickering in the warm breeze.

The people, in desperation
Rake the parched earth
The sun, a ball of fire
Burning in the red-hot sky.

The rose flinched
It glistened in the sun
The pink flower stood alone
The ground was no longer parched
But a puddle of silvery water
Wet to touch.

Katrina Murray (12)
Rugby High School

The Dead Ice Cube

The ice cube was left there,
thrown there like a rag doll, left to die.
Its murderer, big, round and hot,
not caring for its victim.
The dying ice cube was melting,
falling to its death.

It saw most of its life through clear glass,
and now bedded in soft, prickly green stuff,
watching the different feet walk past.
The earth slowly soaking t up . . .
until, there was nothing.

Francesca Mendes (12)
Rugby High School

Forgotten Treasure

Unbearably hot
Dry, desolate, parched
The flowers are gone
The water lilies lie shrivelled on the cracked bed of the river
The sun is a sphere of heat
Longing for the forgotten treasure, water.
Too hot to hope
Too dry to dream
Throat full of flames.
Crying, tears dried up long ago
Evaporated like my dreams of putting out the fire within me.

But then it came
What we had been longing for
Waiting for
And it will never stop.
Drops falling from the cloud-filled expanse we call the sky
The home of the sun.
They pour down
A reflection of beauty
The parched Earth sucks it up, like a sponge
And it quenches my fiery being
Filling the rivers and gifting the water lilies a home again
They fall on my white tongue
The sand becomes mud
All the animals rejoice
And I kneel down, squelching in the mud
And rejoice with them.

Amber Matthews (13)
Rugby High School

Splosh

Earth cracks like a pot,
Hitting the ground with a *crash!*

It was the sun;
The burnt, scorched, body-boiling sun,
That's what it was,
That's what made the parched earth crack.

I wished for a rainbow
To freshen the sky.
I wished for some moisture
To comfort my dry, burnt lips.
But none of those came,
The heat continued on and on.

The land became torrid,
The land became arid,
The land became waterless.

Suddenly, a dark, grey cloud
Filled the sparkling, cobalt blue sky.
There was a rush of relief
From the thirsty villagers.

Out of the blue came a splish,
Next came a splash,
Last came a splat of cool, fresh rain.

This treat dropped from the sky
Like glittering diamonds
From a shattered chandelier.

It was Heaven on Earth.

Alice Pease (12)
Rugby High School

Rainbow

Sky is like a blue sea,
Sparkling, shining.

This is the time of the dreaded heat,
The red-hot sun's glow dries the cracked earth.
Rays still burn on endlessly.

Suddenly in all the heat,
Clouds appear and burst with water,
Hits the ground like glittering metal,
Splish, splosh, splat.
A beautiful rainbow appears,
Glowing different colours.

Fiona Tooke (12)
Rugby High School

Icicles

I couldn't feel my toes,
I felt like crying.
Inside the burning flame
made me glow like a light.

In the mist an oinking pig
trotted by with an icicle tail.
The rain trickled down the window
leaving trails like snails.

In the foggy sky a few grey clouds
floated away,
this happened again and again.

Finally instead of the mist
it was a bright blue, beautiful day.
Villagers came outside
and danced in the fine, sunny day.

Melissa Jordan (12)
Rugby High School

A Light Of Hope

How the longing intensifies,
    The want for warmth is like a stone,
It will always be carried,
    Why, oh why won't the shell of ice break?

Although the warm droplets grow,
    More frequent every day,
The world of melting snow,
    Is not on fast forward.

But then,
    The ice breaks,
A splash of warmth echoes,
    Through the emptiness,
A beam shoots through,
    A light of hope.

How the regret intensifies,
    The want for cold is like a stone,
It will always be carried,
    Why, oh why won't the window of heat crack?

Tegeirian Hutchings (12)
Rugby High School

The Wish For Sun . . .

Raindrops are falling on your head
all the time,
slushy mud,
water lilies are floating,
flowers are drenched.

Imagine, the orange sphere of the sun,
shining down on you for one day,
the reflection in the drying puddles,
like a mirror.

The dark clouds are here
all day and all night.
Now they are spreading,
spreading to let the sun glow upon us,
the sun glows on the land.

The animals are kangaroos,
they're jumping around as if they were springs,
and everyone is singing,
dancing and laughing,
enjoying themselves.

It's hot and the sun looks like a ball of fire
in the blue sky.
Let the sun be here for a while,
Sun god.

Lisa Mehta ((12)
Rugby High School

Water

Water lilies on a dried-up pond,
Wrinkled and dead,
Reflections of a child in the heat,
Staring up into the clear sky,
Waiting for drops.

Then a drop,
Another and another,
And more and more until,
The sky bursts.

And water so good the children scream and run,
And the rain stops but the water carries on,
Flashes of silver buckets,
Empty milk cartons,
And small, cupped hands.

Hayley Marie Kenney (12)
Rugby High School

Shh! It's Not Fair

I heard it, that's how I found out
People were laughing, staring, pointing
I felt sorry for her
Sat in the corner on her own
People were saying that she was a tramp
I wanted to stick up for her
But they'll think I am one of her lot
The teacher didn't do anything
But she sat in the corner and sniggered to herself
It was then when it started and didn't stop.

Sarah Turner (13)
Southam College

The Secret Room

There's a door over there.
No one's ever opened it.
Katie once got quite close,
But heard a scream from within.
She screamed, stumbled, then ran.
Now they have gone and dared me!
I'm walking up slowly,
Reaching out carefully,
Turning it shakily,
Opening it cautiously . . .
Argh!

Rosie Lambert (11)
Southam College

My Friend's Secret

My friend told me a secret,
She said I could not tell,
It was about a boy she knew,
Who wasn't very well.

She said she had to tell someone,
And I was her best friend,
She did seem really worried though,
Could this be his end?

I told her not to worry,
Her secret was safe with me,
The doctors would look after him,
You just wait and see.

I saw her quite soon after,
She came to me and said,
'My friend is getting better,
He's sitting up in bed.'

I said to her the secret
Was more than safe with me,
I'm really glad she's happy now,
That's how best friends should be.

Daisy Harrold (11)
Southam College

Secrets

I have a secret
Do you have a secret?
I have a secret
And one I will not tell

I have a secret
A very big secret
I have a secret
And one I will not tell

I have a secret
A very shocking secret
I have a secret
And one I will not tell

I have a secret
Do you have a secret?
I have a secret
One I did tell.

Adrian van Kesteren (11)
Southam College

Secret Death

They had a fight
And now she's gone
My mum's always crying
I don't know what she's done.

Maybe it's the symbol
Or maybe the god
Just because they're different
Doesn't make them odd.

He came back
And told her what to do
If she didn't do it,
He said, 'I'll shoot you.'

He took me away
To a strange place
He said it doesn't matter
But pulled an odd face.

I knew it was the religion
It must have been
Arguing and fighting
That's all I'd ever seen.

Then the funeral
That I had to miss
Daddy looked down
And gave me a kiss.

Heather Campbell (11)
Southam College

Secrets!

A secret world,
A secret place,
To be all alone there,
To have no care at all,
Get up to what you want,
Get up to anything you please.

I want a secret place,
I wish I had a secret place,
So I can get lost in a world of my own,
So I can be in peace for once.

Secrets can be fun,
Secrets can be hard to keep.

Lauren Case (12)
Southam College

Secrets

I'm sitting here waiting, waiting
For the right person to tell my secret to
Have I found them?
Can you keep a secret?

I'm sitting here waiting, waiting
For the right person to tell my secret to
It's bottled up inside me calling to come out
I need to tell someone, but is that someone you?

I'm sitting here waiting, waiting
For the right person to tell my secret to
If I tell you my secret
Will you keep it safe?

I'm sitting here waiting, waiting
For the right person to tell my secret to
My secret's very special
Shall I tell you?

I'm sitting here waiting, waiting
For the right person to tell my secret to
And that person's you
My secret is . . .
Actually, maybe you're not the right person

I'm sitting here waiting, waiting
For the right person to tell my secret to
And it's not you.

Joanna Green (12)
Southam College

My Secret Garden

I have a secret garden
Which means a lot to me,
I lie beneath the shady trees,
Keeping secrets safe with me.

I close my eyes to dream,
The birds sing in trees above,
I wonder if they have secrets
Or if they fall in love.

A butterfly floats across me,
The colours are very bright,
Does it have secrets too?
Does it think of them in the night?

I hear a shout from behind me,
My secrets I must hide,
I jump up from my leafy bed
And skip merrily inside.

Emma Hill (11)
Southam College

Our Little Secret

We all have secrets,
Just that no one tells.
Here's my secret to you,
But don't blab like bells.

I have a crush
On a famous celeb.
Please keep it hush,
And tell no one else.

His films make me laugh,
And even make me cry.
I'm so in love with him,
I feel like I could fly.

I feel like I could touch the sky,
When I think of him.
In his films I like to see
Him staring alongside Jim.

So this is my secret,
I hope that you won't tell.
Keep it all hush, hush,
So please do not tell.

Jennifer Fennell (13)
Southam College

End Of The World

Hush! Hush! Hush!
You must not tell,
If word gets around,
Then break free will Hell.

This secret holds
The key to the soon,
The world will be dark
And then a red moon.

You will see,
The Devil's wrath,
As unwind,
Will Hell's path.

No joke I will say,
I'm not having a laugh,
Please heed my warning,
Or you'll be cut clean in half.

You fool what have you done?
You've let him loose!
Your curiosity has had you pay
As the world he'll reduce.

An ocean of fire,
So much power,
With his little finger,
Tears down the Eiffel Tower.

Lightning combines,
As the world goes black,
You might as well confess it,
There is no going back.

I saw you tell,
All your mates,
Now none will see,
Heaven's gate.

Callum Moffat (11)
Southam College

Secrets

S ecrets being shared between teachers in the staffroom,
E ntry to the room is getting closer and closer.
C lassroom meetings in silence at break, eager to know
   what they're saying.
R egister's in a minute Miss, quick Miss, quick! Just to have
   a listen to the teachers in the room!
E nter the room, and - *silence!*
T eachers whispering, talking, laughing!

R omantic secrets, secret secrets, anything at all!
O ld people, young people, tell us what you're saying!
O nly if we knew one thing it wouldn't be so bad.
M en, women, talking to themselves.
S isters, brothers, natter, natter, natter!

Tell us what you're saying Miss, please Miss, please?

Annie Allsop (11)
Southam College

Bullying Secret

Wednesday 14th September

I dreaded going to school, to school today. This was the day,
this was the day she was going to get me.
I turned round the corner into school looking cautiously around,
she was going to get me.
All through the day I looked over my shoulder waiting for the moment,
she was going to get me.
She got me. I thought I had got away from her, but I turned round
the corner and she got me. She punched and kicked me,
then ran away leaving me there.

Monday 19th September

I'm so pleased, I did it. I got help, I told a teacher.
I went into school confident that I was going to tell somebody.
I did it. I got help, I told a teacher.

Friday 23rd September

I don't believe it. She came up to me and asked me if I wanted
to be her friend. I'm so happy, I don't believe it.

Alice Thompson Lane (11)
Southam College

A Birthday Wish!

A birthday wish should come true,
For you and me one day it will.
You can wish for a dream to happen today or tomorrow.

When you light the candles
There's a wish in every candle.
The pink sweet icing on the top of the cake
Is as sweet as a nut.
Pink and blue ribbon around the edge.

With a present no wish is made.
A bow on the top and a gift inside,
What can it be?
Let's rip off the ribbon and see.

April Gillett (11)
Southam College

There She Is

There she is,
Strolling down the road.
Going somewhere,
Somewhere dark, damp and cold.

There she is,
In the alleyway.
By the rubbish bins,
And deadly sins.

There she is,
In the local park.
She sits on the swing,
Where the birds never sing.

There she is,
By a shop window,
Looking at her reflection,
It brings no satisfaction.

There she is,
Standing in the road,
A lorry comes by,
There's nothing to do but die.

There she is,
Up in Heaven.
This must be kept a secret,
Forever and ever.

Oh god,
Oh why?

Olivia Ballard (11)
Southam College

Shock

Do you know who I saw
Right outside my front door?
My mouth was open wide,
So wide a mammoth could hide inside.
I'd never seen that person do that before,
It was like to them it was against the law.
I was so shocked, I couldn't breathe,
That spot I could not leave.
I was so frightened,
I thought the world was going to end.
In bed there I lay,
Looking back at the day.
I had acted so stupidly,
But that was sorted out over tea.
Yes, it was Simon Cowell,
With his smile so foul.
I was so scared,
Wouldn't you be?

Jess Pollitt (11)
Southam College

Secrets

Little tin boxes,
Ancient teddy bears,
These are my secrets,
My old shoebox bears.
Shiny marbles glinting bright,
Little metal soldiers marching in the night.
Secrets, secrets, scattered around,
Secrets, secrets, under the ground.
A little toy dog, an American baseball glove,
These are the things that I really love.
Secrets, secrets everywhere,
Secrets, secrets, why are they there?

Luke Ashworth (11)
Southam College

My Secret

I've got a brilliant secret
It's hidden and secure
It's a really special secret
Hidden in a shoe box on my bedroom floor

My secret is a Mars bar hidden in my room
I'm going to sneak up there and eat it very, very soon
But I'll have to be very careful because you see
My mum will get suspicious if I do not want my tea.

Lee Bodfish (12)
Southam College

Secret Of Ghosts

It keeps replaying in my head
All the things that my dad said
But the things that scare me the most
Are the things he said about a ghost.

I kept begging, 'Tell me Dad, please,'
I even sat on my hands and knees
Then he turned around and said to me
He's ginormous, he's 10 foot 3.

He's also got massive fangs
And one of his eyeballs also hangs
Then I said, 'Please Dad stop!'
And covered my face up with my top.

Then I thought of what he said
And what wise words had stuck in my head
Is this the secret you wanted to know
Or would you rather have heard the secret of Pinocchio?

Ricky Jones (12)
Southam College

My Poem!

There?
Where?
Look I'll show you, follow me,
it's on the rotten bench in the park.
There?
Where?
It's jumping on the roof tops
There?
Where?
It's knocking on the vicar's door.
There?
Where?
With the mice and the rats.
There?
Where?
Never mind!

Joanna Middleton (11)
Southam College

The Curse Of Secrets

The whispering of all the room
There's nothing but the boom
The sound of voices; round and round
Why is there so much sound?

The echo goes on and on
No one can go wrong
The teacher screams
We cannot please
But the secrets just go on!

The chatting stops
The buzzing halts
There's not much sound at all
The music from the room next door
Comes buzzing through the walls
And the chatting starts again!

I think the curse of secrets
Approaches us again!

Emily Howell (11)
Southam College

Secrets

The ball was coming straight at me,
My eyes were shut, I could not see.
I heard it whizzing through the air,
Coming closer to my hair.
Hearing shouts from the pitch,
I jumped into the nearest ditch.
Getting up and holding it hard
I made a dash for my backyard.
Once safe inside, with my new ball,
I reflected on my new-found gall.
The players asked the police if the ball had been seen,
To look for it they were really keen.
But the ball I wanted to be my secret,
Hidden away so they would forget.
A ball is something I could not afford,
So the ball had become my new reward.

Jason Heeles (12)
Southam College

Secrets!

I walked into the classroom,
I saw my best friend,
She was sitting with a new girl,
I ran into the girls' toilets,
I started to cry.

I didn't know what to do,
My mind had gone blank,
I just sat there,
On the toilet seat crying.

I waited there,
Till someone came and found me,
No one came for about an hour,
Then I heard a noise,
It sounded like someone was coming in,
I just hid behind the toilet door,
I caught sight of a girl,
It was my best friend.

She saw me peeping behind the cubicle door,
I shut the door quickly,
And hid my hands and face,
I knew I was in trouble,
Then I heard the new girl,
They were talking,
About how they were going to stick together,
What was I going to do on my own?

That was the end of our friendship,
I knew it was,
I heard them go out the toilets,
No need to hide anymore.

Alexandria Kercher (11)
Southam College

My Secret

I have a secret
Will you help?
It's about my best friend
She's smoking and she's twelve.

I caught her on Sunday
Down at the park
She saw me and told me not to tell
But it's so, so hard.

I don't know whether to keep it
Or to tell
I want to keep my best friend though
But I don't want her to go.

It's only been six months
And she's already looking bad
I need someone to tell,
Maybe even your dad.

It's ten years now
She'd be 22
I say 'would' because . . .
She's dead!

Leanne Tarver (11)
Southam College

My Secret

I have got a secret,
I keep it in my head.
When I'm tired and sleepy,
I go there in my bed.

It's a place I think of,
Like Ben Nevis and the Alps.
When I try to go to sleep,
I really think it helps.

It is windy and it's sunny,
The sun is in my face.
It is always nice to rest there,
When I'm in my secret place.

I like the peace upon my mountain
With the bleating of the sheep,
And with no one there to bother me
It means that I can sleep.

Jethro Lomas (11)
Southam College

Secrets

It's hard to keep a secret,
Shall I tell my mum?
It's hard to keep a secret,
I need to tell someone.

Should I tell my best friend,
Or my brother Jake?
Oh, decisions, decisions,
What a tough choice to make.

It's hard to keep a secret,
I told no one at all.
It's hard to keep a secret,
So I wrote it on the wall.

Toby Tomlinson (11)
Southam College

The Forest Of Nightmares

Tarantulas swarm like black clouds
Jump out and attack with venomous fangs
Like long, strong daggers
Beware of giant venomous tarantulas
Snakes hiss aggressively
They come and squeeze you with their strength
Hiding under bark in the forest
Snakes come out like strong, long worms
Wasps swarm like black and yellow clouds
Mosquitoes buzz aggressively to bite your skin painfully;
To suck your salty blood
Massive fungus-like mushrooms pop poisonously
The trees were sporting bracket, fungus-like giant
Luminous, rubbery hands.

I wake in a petrified way
I go to the bathroom for a wash and a drink of water
I feel sick with relief
I look in the mirror, phew!
I'm glad I'm back to normal.

But what is this?
A hairy leg of a black widow spider
Crawls out of my ear and across my face
And I'm back in horror in the dark of the Forest of Nightmares.

James Handford (13)
Sparrowdale School

Trains

Trains that talk to you
Mustn't be late . . . mustn't be late
High speed trains
Slow trains
Noisy trains
Never early trains.

Trains that talk to you
Have to go faster . . . have to go faster
Sonic trains
Bionic trains
Turbo trains
Got to get there trains.

Trains that talk to you
What a beautiful day . . . what a beautiful day
Trees that pass in a blur
Houses that blend
Blue sky, grey sky
Get to the destination trains.

Michael Cox (13)
Sparrowdale School

Goldfish

They swim all day
Blowing bubbles all day
They suck food all day
Their gills flap all day
Their eyes glare all day
Their tails flick all day
They float all day
They look out of their bowl all day
They look out for cats all day
They glitter all day
They are slimy all day
And they sleep all night.

Shane Bibb (13)
Sparrowdale School

Pop Idol Hero

His spiky hair excites me.
He's my pop idol.
His smile touches my heart.
He's handsome like a pop idol.
I like his voice it makes me relax every time I hear it.
His songs are great, make me want to dance.
He's in my dreams every time I sleep.
I've got pictures of him on my wall.
My hero is Gareth Gates.

Danielle Gallett (13)
Sparrowdale School

Best Friend

Best friends are helpful.
Best friends keep secrets.
Best friends look after you when you're upset.
Best friends are always there for you.
Best friends share their tuck with you.
Best friends share their thoughts with you.
Best friends play with you at break time.
Best friends giggle at the same things.
Best friends sleep over at your house.
Best friends say, 'Well done' when you've done good work.
Best friends choose you for their team in games.
Where would I be without my best friend?

Jenna Passey (13)
Sparrowdale School

Dolphins

Dolphins are in the water
Dolphins are soft
Dolphins are smooth
Dolphins have sharp teeth
Dolphins are grey
Dolphins are bottle-nosed creatures
Dolphins are smooth swimmers
Dolphins ride in the waves
Dolphins are friendly
Dolphins turn in the water
Dolphins are cute
Dolphins dive deeply in the water
Dolphins are the best creatures.

Sarah O'Reilly (13)
Sparrowdale School

My Pony John

My pony is small and grey
His coat is soft
His tail is long and grey
He swishes the flies away
My pony can walk, canter and gallop
His hooves go *clip-clop*
I like to ride my pony John
When the weather is nice.

Sabrina Parker (13)
Sparrowdale School

Puppies

Four little puppies waiting for a new home
Three little puppies waiting for a new home
Two little puppies waiting for a new home
One little puppy waiting for a new home.

Wait a minute . . .

Where have all the puppies gone?
Oh don't worry, they're only playing hide-and-seek.

Sara Bibb (13)
Sparrowdale School

The Big Black Spider

Spinning a web,
Walking around with its hairy great legs.
Here he comes,
Oh, what is that?
I see my little friend, my prey.
Stay there little bluebottle.
I'm coming for you.
Eight-legged freak is ready to pounce.
Here I come for my fly dinner.
Wing, bread and butter.

Tom Betteridge (14)
Sparrowdale School